I0643760

Waves: Light and Sound

Sound Waves

Robin Johnson and Priyanka Das

LIGHTBOX
openlightbox.com

LIGHTBOX

Go to
www.openlightbox.com
and enter this book's
unique code.

ACCESS CODE

LBXZ8879

Lightbox is an all-inclusive digital solution for the teaching and learning of curriculum topics in an original, groundbreaking way. Lightbox is based on National Curriculum Standards.

OPTIMIZED FOR

- ✓ TABLETS
- ✓ WHITEBOARDS
- ✓ COMPUTERS
- ✓ AND MUCH MORE!

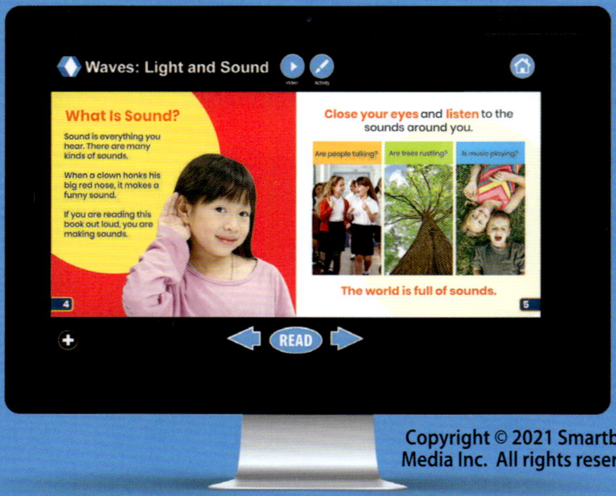

Copyright © 2021 Smartbook Media Inc. All rights reserved.

STANDARD FEATURES OF LIGHTBOX

AUDIO High-quality narration using text-to-speech system

VIDEOS Embedded high-definition video clips

ACTIVITIES Printable PDFs that can be emailed and graded

WEBLINKS Curated links to external, child-safe resources

SLIDESHOWS Pictorial overviews of key concepts

INTERACTIVE MAPS Interactive maps and aerial satellite imagery

QUIZZES Ten multiple choice questions that are automatically graded and emailed for teacher assessment

KEY WORDS Matching key concepts to their definitions

VIDEOS

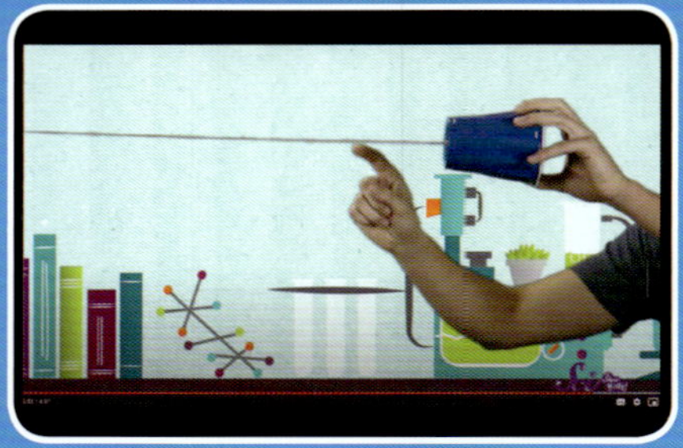

WEBLINKS

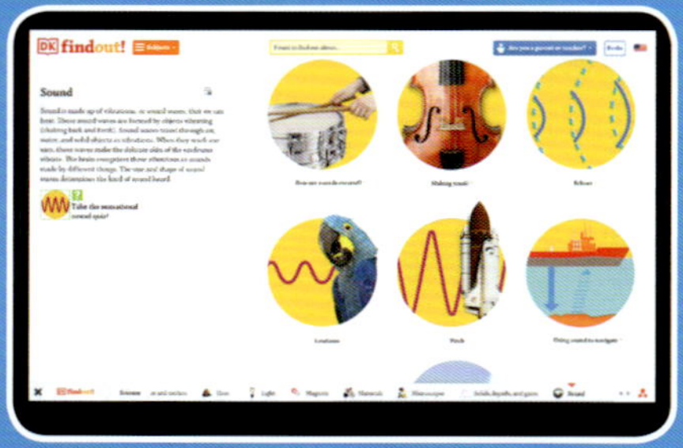

SLIDESHOWS

QUIZZES

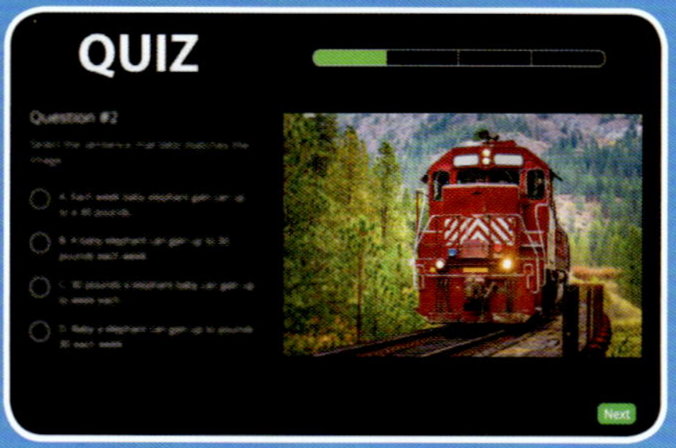

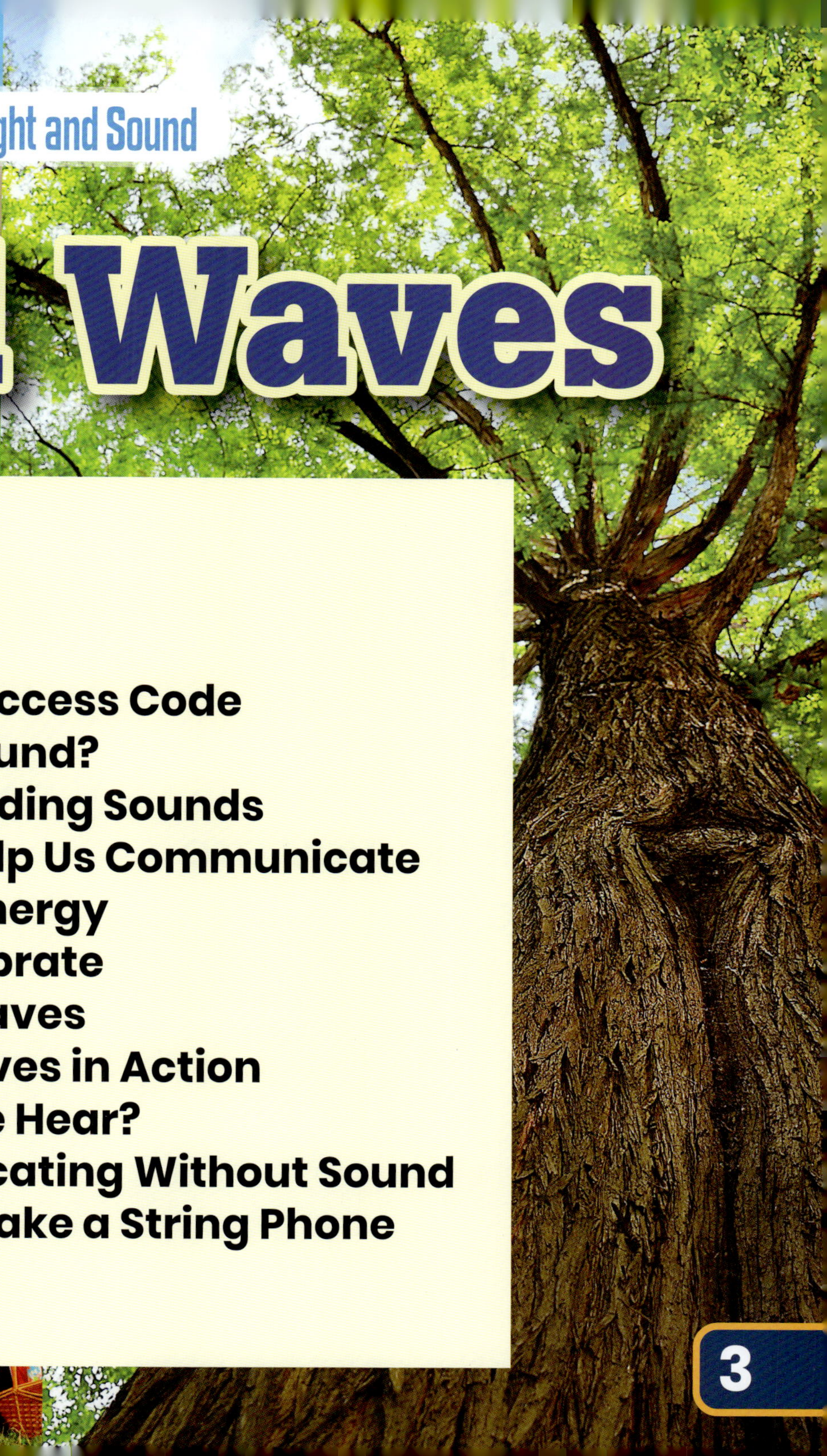

Sound Waves

Contents

What Is Sound?

Sound is everything you hear. There are many kinds of sounds.

When a clown honks his big red nose, it makes a funny sound.

If you are reading this book out loud, you are making sounds.

Close your eyes and **listen** to the sounds around you.

Are people talking?

Are leaves rustling?

Is music playing?

The world is full of sounds.

Understanding Sounds

Sounds are an important part of life. They help you understand the world around you.

Have you ever heard an ambulance siren? It tells you help is on the way to someone who is in trouble.

Sounds can warn **people and animals** of **danger**.

The ringing of a fire alarm means there might be a fire. It tells you to leave the building.

A beaver may slap its big, flat tail on the water. This makes a splashing sound. It warns other beavers that there might be danger.

Sounds Help Us Communicate

People and animals use sounds to communicate. To communicate is to share ideas and information. Most people communicate by talking. You whisper secrets in your friend's ear. You shout if someone is far away.

Sounds can also show **feelings**.

You giggle when you are happy.

Babies cry when they are hungry.

Dogs growl when they are angry or scared.

Sound Is Energy

Sound is a form of energy. You need energy to move, play, and talk. You even need energy to learn about sound! Sound is energy that you can hear.

Sound travels more than **10 times faster** than a **cheetah**.

Objects Vibrate

Sound is only made when objects vibrate. To vibrate is to shake. Vibrating objects move quickly back and forth. Sometimes, the movements are too small to see or feel.

Try picking guitar strings with your fingers. You will see them vibrate. The moving strings make music sounds.

All objects **vibrate** and make **sound**.

When you knock on a door, the door vibrates.

A bouncing ball vibrates.

A ringing phone vibrates.

Making Waves

Sound travels in waves. When an object vibrates, sound waves are created. The waves travel away from the object. They reach your ears. This is how you hear.

New York City is one of the loudest cities in the United States.

Volume is how **loud** or **quiet** a sound is.

A strong vibration has more energy. It makes a loud sound. Trains are very loud.

A vibration with less energy makes a soft sound. Butterflies flap their wings quietly.

Sound Waves in Action

Vibrating objects make sound.
Sound can also make objects vibrate.

Loud sounds have a lot of energy.
They give off strong vibrations.
These vibrations can move objects.
They may rattle windows. They may
even shake the ground!

Airplanes make a loud "Boom!" noise.
This can feel like a small earthquake.

You can see **sound waves** in **action**.

Try taping a piece of paper to the front of a speaker. Turn the music up. Sound waves will make the paper jump!

You can also sing a tune to feel sound. Put your fingers on your throat while you sing. Do you feel the vibrations?

How Do We Hear?

Ears catch sound waves as they pass by. The waves enter the outer ear. They travel down the ear canal. Then, they hit the eardrum. The eardrum is a thin flap of skin. It vibrates when sound waves hit it.

Sound travels from your **ear** to your **brain**.

There are tiny bones in the middle of the ear. They vibrate when the eardrum vibrates.

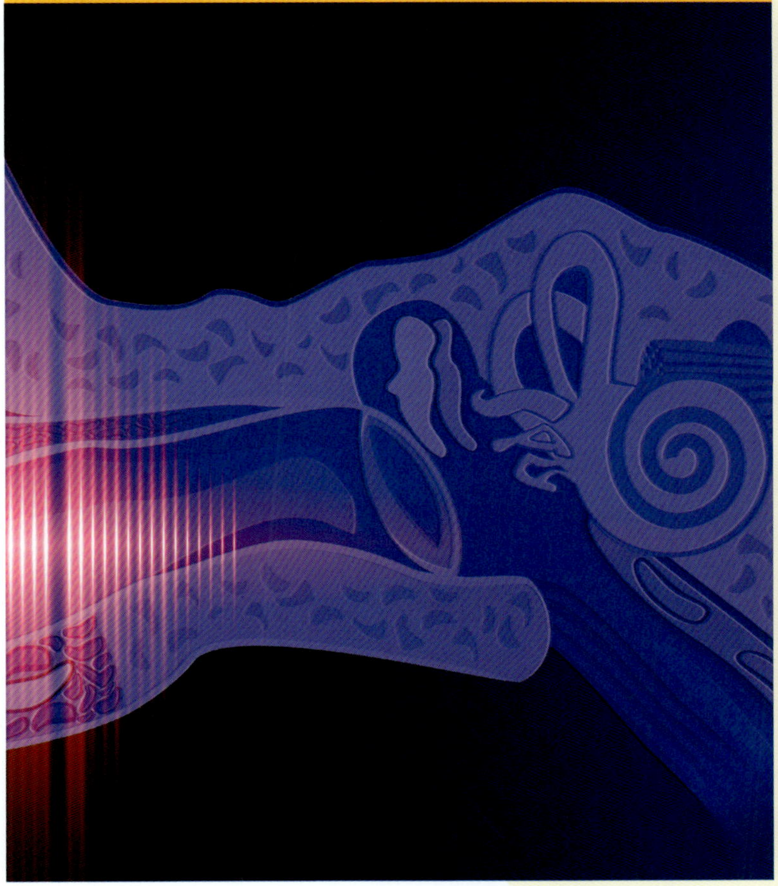

The sound signals get carried to your brain. Your brain tells you what you are hearing.

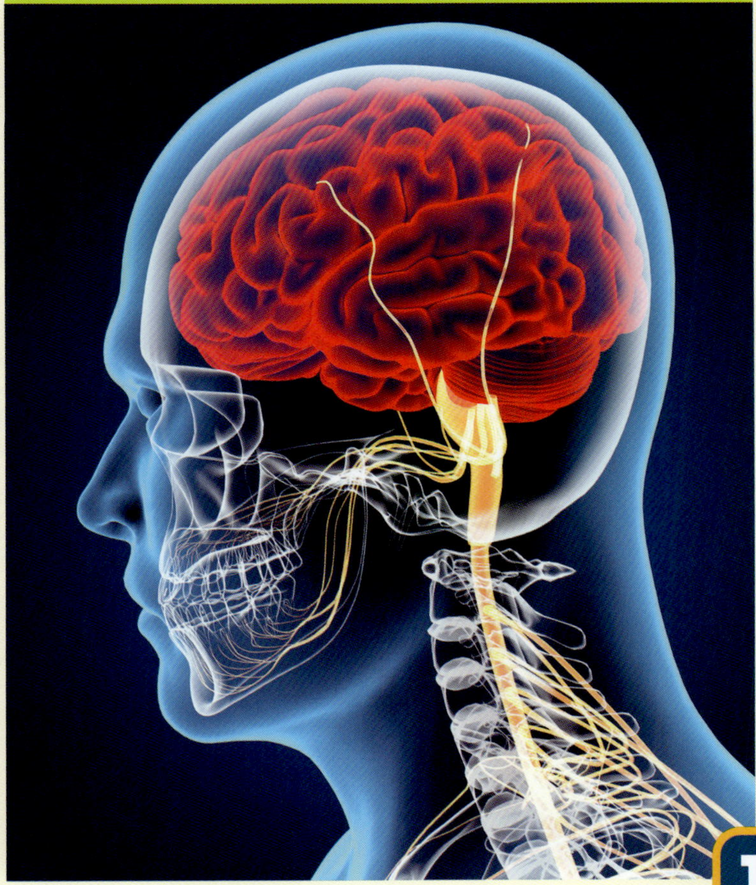

Communicating Without Sound

Some people cannot hear very well. Others do not hear sounds at all. These people are deaf. Many deaf people communicate without sound. They use sign languages instead.

Spoken languages use sound. English is a spoken language. A sign language uses hand movements. It is understood through the eyes. There are many sign languages. American Sign Language (ASL) is used in the United States.

Nearly **1 in 20 Americans** is deaf or hard of hearing.

Activity

Make a String Phone

Telephones let you communicate over a distance. You can make your own phone. Then, call your friends!

Supplies

String

Two paper cups

Scissors

STEP 1 Cut a long piece of string.

STEP 2 Make a small hole in the bottom of each paper cup.

STEP 3 Poke one end of the string through each hole. Tie a knot on each end of the string inside the cups. Now, the string cannot slip out.

STEP 4 Hold one cup. Ask a friend to take the other cup. Pull the cups apart gently. The string should be stretched tightly.

STEP 5 Speak into one cup. Have your friend put the other cup to his ear. His brain tells him what you said. Then, listen while your friend speaks into the cup.

KEY WORDS

Research has shown that as much as 65 percent of all written material published in English is made up of 300 words. These 300 words cannot be taught using pictures or learned by sounding them out. They must be recognized by sight. This book contains 117 common sight words to help young readers improve their reading fluency and comprehension. This book also teaches young readers several important content words, such as proper nouns. These words are paired with pictures to aid in learning and improve understanding.

Page	Sight Words First Appearance
4	a, are, big, book, hear, his, if, is, it, kinds, makes, many, of, out, sound, there, this, what, when, you
5	and, around, close, eyes, leaves, people, the, to, world, your
6	an, have, help, important, in, life, on, part, tells, they, way, who
7	animals, be, can, its, may, means, might, other, that, water
8	away, by, far, ideas, most, us, use
9	also, or, show
10	about, even, learn, move, need, play, talk
11	more, than, times
12	back, made, only, see, small, sometimes, them, too, try, will, with
13	all
14	city, from, how, new, one, states
15	has, their, very
16	give, like, off, these
17	do, paper, put, turn, up, while
18	as, down, then, we
19	get
20	American, at, hand, not, some, through, well, without
21	hard

Page	Content Words First Appearance
4	clown, nose
5	music
6	ambulance siren, trouble
7	beaver, building, danger, fire alarm, tail
8	ear, friend, information, secrets
9	babies, dogs, feelings
10	energy
11	cheetah
12	fingers, guitar strings, movements, objects
13	ball, door, phone
14	New York City, United States, waves
15	butterflies, trains, vibration, volume, wings
16	action, airplanes, earthquake, ground, noise, windows
17	piece, speaker, throat
18	ear canal, eardrum, flap, outer ear, skin
19	bones, brain, middle, signals
20	American Sign Language (ASL), deaf, English, movements, sign languages, spoken languages

Published by Smartbook Media Inc.
14 Penn Plaza, 9th Floor New York, NY 10122
Website: www.openlightbox.com

Copyright ©2021 Smartbook Media Inc.
All rights reserved. No part of this publication may be reproduced, stored in a retrieval system, or transmitted in any form or by any means, electronic, mechanical, photocopying, recording, or otherwise, without the prior written permission of the publisher.

Library of Congress Control Number: 2020937079

ISBN 978-1-5105-5408-5 (hardcover)
ISBN 978-1-5105-5409-2 (multi-user eBook)

Printed in Guangzhou, China
1 2 3 4 5 6 7 8 9 0 24 23 22 21 20

052020
110819

Project Coordinator: Priyanka Das
Designer: Jean Faye Marie Rodriguez

Every reasonable effort has been made to trace ownership and to obtain permission to reprint copyright material. The publisher would be pleased to have any errors or omissions brought to its attention so that they may be corrected in subsequent printings.

The publisher acknowledges iStock and Shutterstock as the primary image suppliers for this title.

First published by Crabtree Publishing Company in 2014.